AMERIGO VESPUCCI

AMERIGO VESPUCCI

Dennis Brindell Fradin

FRANKLIN WATTS
New York • London • Toronto • Sydney
A First Book • 1991

Frontispiece: Amerigo Vespucci used an astrolabe and other astronomical instruments to chart the movements of the moon and other celestial bodies.

Cover photograph courtesy of Historical Pictures Service, Chicago

Photographs courtesy of: Art Resource Inc., N.Y.: pp. 47 (Giraudon), 14, 15, 23 (all Scala); The Bettmann Archive: pp. 2, 8, 17, 20, 22, 40 top, 50, 56; Historical Pictures Service, Chicago: pp. 11, 30, 34 top, 42; New York Public Library, Picture Collection: pp. 18, 40 bottom; Ronald Sheridan/Ancient Art and Architecture Collection: pp. 26, 29, 32, 34 bottom, 52; The Pierpont Morgan Library, N.Y., N.Y.: p. 38 (M.525,F.17).

Library of Congress Cataloging-in-Publication Data

Fradin, Dennis B.
Amerigo Vespucci / Dennis Brindell Fradin.
p.   cm.—(A First book)
Includes bibliographical references and index.
Summary: Traces the life of the famed Florentine explorer who discovered Brazil, Venezuela, and the Amazon River, and had two continents named for him.
ISBN 0-531-20035-3
1. Vespucci, Amerigo, 1451–1512—Juvenile literature.
2. Explorers—America—Biography—Juvenile literature.
3. Explorers—Spain—Biography—Juvenile literature.   4. Explorers—Portugal—Biography—Juvenile literature.   5. America—Discovery and exploration—Spanish—Juvenile literature.   6. America—Discovery and exploration—Portuguese—Juvenile literature.
[1. Vespucci, Amerigo, 1451–1512.   2. Explorers.   3. America—Discovery and exploration—Spanish.]   I. Title.   II. Series.
E125.V5F7   1991
970.01′6′092—dc20
[B]   91-14748   CIP   AC

For my wonderful and beautiful niece,
Lauren Michelle Bloom,
from Uncle Dennis with love

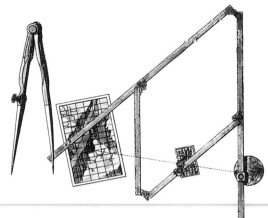

CONTENTS

**Amerigo Vespucci (1454–1512), in a sixteenth-
century engraving, holds a map of the
New World he helped to explore.**

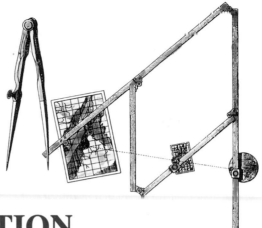

INTRODUCTION

IF YOU HAD a penny for every time the word "America" is said, sung, written, or read in a day, you would be very rich. People in the United States of America say the word while reciting the pledge of allegiance to the flag. They say it while singing "America the Beautiful" and other patriotic songs. The word "America" also appears on our money. Many people in the United States of America shorten this name and call their nation America and refer to themselves as Americans.

In the main meaning of the word, though, America refers to a much larger region than just the United States. It refers to two of the earth's large landmasses, known as continents. One of these continents is North America, on which such countries as Canada, the United States, and Mexico are located. The other is South America, on which Brazil, Peru, Argentina, and other countries are found. Altogether, nearly a billion people, or about a seventh of the world's population, live in North and South America. Many of them speak Spanish and call the continents Norte América and Sud América. Many others speak French and call them Amérique du Nord and Amérique du Sud.

Few people in the Americas know much about the man for whom their continents were named. The word "America" is a variation of the first name of the Italian explorer Amerigo Vespucci, who reached the New World at least twice around the year 1500. Within a few years, map makers and then the general public began calling the lands he had visited America. This name was maintained, even though some people wanted to call the lands Columbia or Columba after Christopher Columbus, the famous explorer who first reached the New World in 1492.

The name America was chosen over Columbia and Columba for two reasons. The main one was that Amerigo Vespucci was the first person to understand the nature of the lands that he and Columbus had visited. Columbus had been trying to reach Asia when he reached

The galleon, as seen here, was among the sailing ships used by explorers of the fifteenth century.

the Americas in 1492, and for the rest of his life he claimed he had been to Asia. Amerigo realized that the landmass across the Atlantic Ocean was a region that had been previously unknown to Europeans.

Anyone who has ever said or sung the word "America" can understand the second reason it prevailed. The name is very beautiful. The people of the early 1500s loved its musical sound, and this helped America to be chosen over Columbia, Columba, and other suggestions.

CHAPTER I

AMERIGO'S
EARLY YEARS

IN March of 1454, in what is now the city of Florence, Italy, a baby was born into the Vespucci family. He was named Amerigo after his father's father. Italy was not yet a single nation. Instead, it contained many city-states such as Genoa, Venice, Pisa, and Florence. These city-states were much like independent nations. The grand-father for whom little Amerigo had been named was one of Florence's leading officials. The boy's father, Nasta-gio Vespucci, was also an important public official in Florence. Little Amerigo had two older brothers, and later a younger brother and a younger sister. Little is known about Amerigo's mother, Elisabetta Vespucci, except that she seemed to pay the most attention to her oldest child, Antonio. As adults, Amerigo and one of his brothers complained in letters to each other that their mother "lived for Antonio."

FIORENZA

A map of Florence in 1490 shows the beautiful, exciting city-state where Amerigo was born.

Amerigo lived in one of the most exciting cities during one of history's most exciting periods. For hundreds of years between about the year A.D. 400 and A.D. 1300, Europeans had shown little interest in the pursuit of knowledge. Because of this, those centuries are sometimes called the Dark Ages. From the 1300s until about 1600, however, Europeans displayed a renewed interest in learning and art. This period is called Europe's Renaissance, a word that means rebirth.

During the Renaissance, the astronomer Nicolaus Copernicus revealed that the earth was not the center of the universe, the doctor Andreas Vesalius learned many facts about the human body, artists such as Leonardo da Vinci and Michelangelo created some of the world's greatest paintings and sculptures, and explorers made many important discoveries.

As one of the leading centers of the Renaissance, Florence in Amerigo Vespucci's time was home to a large number of people who made their mark on history. Amerigo and his family knew most of those great Flor-

Nicolaus Copernicus, an astronomer of Vespucci's time, made observations of the sun, moon, and planets, and worked out a system showing that the planets revolved around the sun.

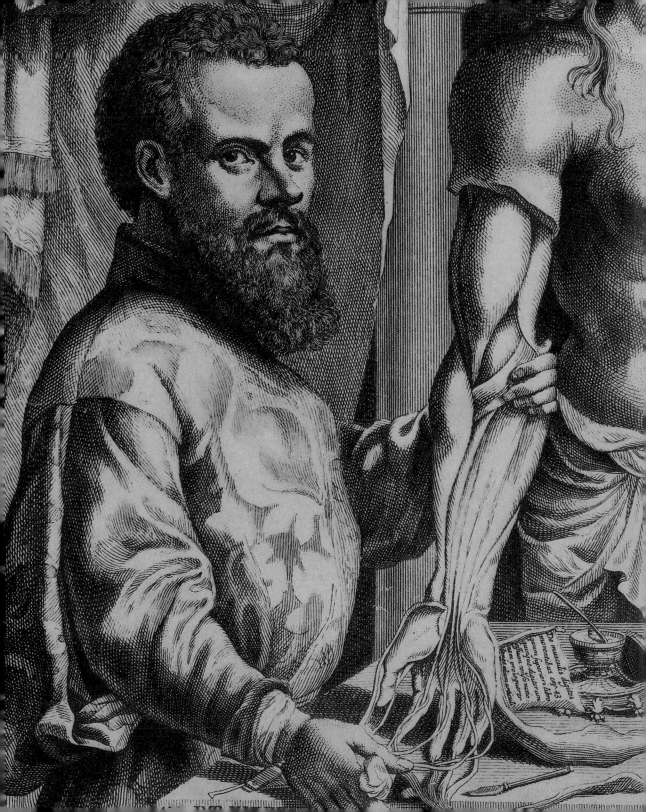

cntines, including the artists Leonardo da Vinci, Sandro Botticelli, and Andrea del Verrocchio. Leonardo once spent all day following Amerigo's grandfather around Florence to fix his features in his mind. He then went home and drew a sketch of the old man. Botticelli used a cousin of Amerigo's as a model for his famous painting *Birth of Venus*. Verrocchio lived in a house belonging to one of the Vespuccis.

The family also knew the great political writer Niccolò Machiavelli. Florence was home to only about 30,000 people in Amerigo's day. Because the city was so small, the prominent Vespucci family may also have known Michelangelo and many other famous Florentines.

Their concern for education was one reason so many Florentines achieved greatness. Education in those days was not the kind of education we have today. Instead of going to school, young craftsmen and artists learned by working for older men, experts who taught them everything they knew. For example, Leonardo da Vinci worked and studied with Andrea del Verrocchio for a few years before opening his own studio. Many wealthier young

Andreas Vesalius, another Renaissance scientist, studied the human body.

19

A later painter portrayed the great Renaissance artist Michelangelo in his studio, surrounded by his works, receiving a visit from Pope Julius II.

Florentines studied with private tutors. In some cases they then went on to the University of Pisa or to another of Italy's fine universities.

Near the time of Amerigo's birth, a great breakthrough in book publishing began to revolutionize education. During the early 1440s, Johannes Gutenberg of Germany began printing books with a press that used movable type. This new method of producing books by machine enabled printers to create hundreds of copies of a book per day. Before this, it had taken many days to copy a single book by hand. Because printed books were less expensive and more plentiful than the handwritten books they replaced, they helped to spread the ideas of the Renaissance throughout Europe.

Amerigo, as one of the wealthier young Florentines, studied with a private tutor. His teacher was his uncle, the priest Giorgio Antonio Vespucci. Using books from his own large library as texts, Uncle Giorgio taught Amerigo Latin, mathematics, astronomy, and literature. He also showed his nephew maps of the known world and introduced him to Florence's leading thinkers.

The composition book that Amerigo wrote in while being taught by his Uncle Giorgio still exists. In it Amerigo wrote that he was willing to "endure all fatigue" if only he could do something that would "win fame and honor." His compositions also show that from

Gutenberg and his assistants examine his first proof
sheet, produced on his invention—a
printing press that used movable type.

A world map from about 1460 shows the
world as known and charted
before Amerigo Vespucci's time.

an early age he had a thirst for learning, an open mind, and a desire to discover the truth about things. These traits enabled Amerigo to make a discovery later in life that won him this great "fame and honor."

Except for his education, we know little about Amerigo's early years. One of the few stories about his youth concerns an event that reportedly occurred in the village of Peretola, about 6 miles (about 10 km) outside Florence. Amerigo and his family sometimes visited two uncles who owned an inn in Peretola. One day, according to the story which has been told around Peretola for centuries, Amerigo's father and uncles told him to leave the room while they discussed adult matters. Later, when they looked for Amerigo, they couldn't find him around the inn or in the nearby fields. Just when Amerigo's family decided that he must have run away, they found him sitting on a hilltop. Amerigo explained that he had just wanted to look at the sky.

Amerigo's composition book shows that he was serious and scholarly even when young. The story about him sitting on the hilltop is often told to show that Amerigo also had a little of the poet or the daydreamer about him. Whether or not this story is true, Amerigo really did have a touch of the poet about him. This is evident in the detailed descriptions of America he was to write later in his life.

While still a young man, Amerigo apparently made a trip to Rome with his uncle Giorgio, although the nature of this visit is unknown. At the age of twenty-five, Amerigo accompanied another relative on a political mission to Paris, France. But aside from these journeys and some short business trips, Amerigo wasn't much of a traveler until well past his fortieth birthday. He was a successful businessman who liked to study geography books and maps as a hobby.

For several years, Amerigo worked as a businessman with his father. Then, in the spring of 1482, Nastagio Vespucci died. Although Amerigo's three brothers had attended the University of Pisa, none of them was in a position to earn much money. Amerigo became his family's main breadwinner.

In 1483, the year after Nastagio Vespucci's death, Amerigo went to work for the Medicis, Florence's leading family. For nearly ten years, Amerigo lived in the home of two Medici brothers. He did everything from managing their banking business to selling their crops. Dozens of letters written to Amerigo during these years reveal that he was one of the most respected men in Florence. He supported several members of his family and helped many other people get started in business. And Amerigo repaid the Medicis' trust by earning a great deal of money for them.

**Amerigo's employers were the
wealthy and powerful Medici
family. Shown here is
Lorenzo de' Medici, far right.**

Something happened in late 1491 that was to shape the rest of Amerigo's life. The Medicis asked him to go to Seville, Spain, to see if a business contact was cheating them. Amerigo went to Cádiz, Spain, in early 1492 and then moved to nearby Seville a few months later. He loved Seville so much that he made it his home for the rest of his life. In Spain, Amerigo worked as a business agent for the Medicis and also as an independent merchant who helped fit out ships.

CHAPTER II

AMERIGO AND CHRISTOPHER COLUMBUS

FOR SOMEONE who liked geography, Spain, and especially the Seville area, was a very exciting place during the early 1490s. At that time, Europeans wanted to find a good route to Asia, where they hoped to obtain gold, spices, and other treasures. Traveling to Asia over land routes was very difficult and dangerous. Most people thought the best way to reach Asia would be to sail south and then east around Africa.

In the late 1480s, just several years before Amerigo's arrival in Spain, Bartholomeu Dias of nearby Portugal had become the first known European to sail around the Cape of Good Hope near Africa's southern tip. Dias had wanted to continue around Africa all the way to Asia, but exhaustion and a dwindling food supply had forced his expedition to return to Portugal. Nevertheless, many people in Portugal and Spain felt that men would

The Portugese navigator Bartholomeu Dias sailed with two vessels around the Cape of Good Hope, trying to find a passage from Europe to Asia.

Another Portugese navigator, Vasco da Gama,
led the first successful voyage from Europe
around Africa to Asia, and was received
by the ruler of Calcut (Calcutta).

soon sail all the way around Africa to Asia. This was done by Vasco da Gama of Portugal a few years later in 1497–1498.

There was a man in Spain, though, who had a totally different plan for reaching Asia. This man, an Italian sailor named Christopher Columbus, claimed that Asia could be reached by sailing about 3,000 miles (5,000 km) west across the Atlantic Ocean. In one way, Columbus's idea made sense. Educated people of the time knew that the earth was round, which meant that any spot on the planet could be reached from the east or the west if one went far enough. However, many geographers disagreed with Columbus's idea of the earth's size. They claimed that the world was much larger and that Asia was much farther away than Columbus believed.

These experts were right and Columbus was wrong. In addition, two continents that were unknown to Europeans blocked the path to Asia. These were the continents later named for Amerigo Vespucci. Columbus was very confident about his plan, though, and so he and his brother went from country to country asking kings and queens to pay for a westward voyage to Asia. Columbus's plan was rejected in Portugal, England, and France, but his main efforts were in Spain, where he spent over five years seeking help from Queen Isabella and King Ferdinand.

Columbus's persistence was finally rewarded. In

Christopher Columbus hoped to reach Asia by a different route—by sailing west across the Atlantic.

January of 1492, around the time Amerigo arrived in Spain, Isabella and Ferdinand promised to send Columbus on a westward voyage to Asia later that year.

A business friend of Amerigo's helped fit out Columbus's ships, the *Niña,* the *Pinta,* and the *Santa María.* This man may have introduced Amerigo to Christopher before the Columbus expedition sailed, or perhaps after it returned. In any case, we know that Christopher and Amerigo became friends.

On August 3, 1492, Columbus departed on his great voyage from a town near Seville. His three ships averaged about 100 miles (160 km) per day on their westward journey. By early October, Columbus's men were begging him to return home. They thought they would die of hunger or thirst before reaching Asia. Columbus finally promised that they would head home if they didn't reach land within three days. At 2 A.M. on October 12, 1492, not long before the time would have expired, the *Pinta*'s lookout spotted land. Columbus had reached the Bahamas, southeast of Florida. Although separated from the mainland by water, these islands are considered part of North America.

Columbus's arrival in the Bahamas didn't mean that he had discovered the Americas, as many people think. Around A.D. 1000, the Viking explorer Leif Eriksson had landed in an unknown part of North America. Knowledge of Eriksson's exploration was lost in Columbus's

Before Vespucci and Columbus, Leif Eriksson is believed to have led a Viking expedition to America around A.D. 1000.

A sixteenth-century artist showed a group of natives greeting Columbus on Hispaniola, with his three-ship fleet behind him in the harbor.

and Amerigo's time, but we know about it today. It also appears that black West Africans had reached America by canoe a number of times before Columbus's arrival. What Columbus did do was open the way for the colonization of the Americas. Shiploads of Spanish settlers moved to the islands off Florida's coast over the next few years.

In addition to the Bahamas, Columbus explored the islands of Hispaniola (on which Haiti and the Dominican Republic are now located) and Cuba on his famous 1492 voyage. Had Columbus been more open-minded, he would have known that he wasn't in Asia. For one thing, where were the great Asian cities? For another, why didn't the natives look the way Asians had been described? But Columbus wanted to believe that he had reached Asia. He decided that Cuba was China and that Hispaniola was Japan. The great cities, he reasoned, were a short way from the regions he had explored. As for the people, he concluded that some Asians looked different than people had claimed. At the time, Asian lands in the region of India, Japan, and China were called the Indies. Certain that he had reached the Indies, Columbus called the natives Indians.

Columbus kidnapped some Indians and obtained some gold in the islands, then headed home. People were amazed to see Columbus and his crew when they reached Spain in the spring of 1493. They had been gone for more than seven months, and it was thought that they all might have died at sea.

Christopher Columbus was welcomed as a hero. Everyone wanted to hear about his explorations and see the Indians. Those who saw the Indians agreed with Columbus that some Asians looked different than had been thought. Over the next few years, Ferdinand and Isabella sent Columbus back to the "Indies" three times to explore more, build settlements, and look for gold. Amerigo Vespucci helped Columbus prepare for his second (1493–96) and his third voyages (1498–1500). Soon after Columbus made his third trip across the Atlantic Ocean, Amerigo left on an exploring voyage of his own.

CHAPTER III

AMERIGO'S FIRST KNOWN VOYAGE

THE BELIEF in Spain was that Columbus had reached Asia's outer islands. Spain still hoped to reach the Asian mainland by a westward voyage. In the spring of 1499, a fleet of either four or six ships under Alonso de Hojeda sailed from Spain, partly to search for mainland Asia. Amerigo Vespucci, who was then forty-five years old, went on this voyage. We don't know how it happened that this middle-aged merchant decided to cross the ocean. We can't even be sure that this was Amerigo's first voyage, although most historians think it was.

Amerigo had a dual role on this voyage. In those days, sailors studied the positions of stars to help determine their course at sea. Since Amerigo knew a lot about astronomy, he was to help Alonso de Hojeda navigate. He also served as the representative of merchants who hoped to find ways of striking it rich in Asia.

Nicolao coelho

Jao. frz

Pedraluez cabral·

Symao Demjrao Bo

Duqus de figujro

Bertolameu Diaz

Thanks to a letter that Amerigo later wrote to one of the Medicis, we know many details about this voyage. The expedition left Cádiz, Spain, on May of 1499. Alonso de Hojeda was more interested in finding pearls than in exploring, while Amerigo viewed it as a "voyage of discovery." Because of this, once in the Atlantic Ocean Amerigo was allowed to break away with two ships and follow his own course westward. Amerigo sailed farther south than Alonso de Hojeda, toward a region that wasn't yet explored. Helped by good winds, Amerigo's ships covered the 3,700 miles (6,000 km) in just about a month, arriving at what is now the eastern coast of Brazil in South America around June 27, 1499. Amerigo and his men had become the first known Europeans to reach Brazil.

Amerigo sailed southward along Brazil's coast, reaching a distance of more than 300 miles (500 km) below the equator, the imaginary line that encircles the earth's middle between its northern and southern hemi-

Among the sailing expeditions that set out to explore the New World was one led by Pedro Alvares Cabral in 1500, as shown in this record book of the period.

This drawing of explorers reaching land in the New World appeared in a 1505 book of Amerigo's letters describing his voyages.

Amerigo's explorations along the coast of South America and discoveries by other explorers provided the information for European mapmakers of the New World, as seen in this 1540 map.

spheres. Then he headed north and west along the South American coast all the way to Venezuela.

In addition to becoming the first explorer to reach Brazil, Amerigo achieved several other firsts and made several discoveries along the South American coast. He was the first known explorer to cross south of the equator in the Americas. He is believed to have discovered two important South American rivers, the Amazon and the Pará. He also named the country of Venezuela, which is Spanish for "Little Venice." He chose that name because it reminded him of the Italian city of Venice. Amerigo made what was probably his greatest discovery of this voyage while watching the stars night after night from the deck of his ship.

For many years, sailors had known how to figure the distance they had traveled north or south. They did it by measuring the height of the North Star, which is situated almost exactly over earth's North Pole. The farther north one travels, the higher the North Star appears in the sky. The farther south one goes, the lower the North Star appears. In Amerigo's time, sailors used instruments called the *astrolabe* and the *quadrant* to measure the North Star's height. But sailors could not accurately figure the distance they had traveled east or west until Amerigo found a way to do this during his 1499 voyage.

Amerigo's method was very complicated. It involved measuring and timing certain movements of the

**Amerigo's descriptions of his voyages
were later printed as a book.**

moon. By comparing his results to what they would be back in Europe, he was able to determine how far west he had gone. Amerigo's system of determining east-west position was used by sailors and explorers for the next 250 years.

His writings reveal that Amerigo loved the sights and smells of the South American coast. The trees were so thick "that a bird could scarcely fly through them," Amerigo wrote. They also smelled wonderful. He was amazed by the beauty of the tropical birds, some of which "were a brilliant scarlet [bright red]; others green spotted with lemon; others all green; still others black and flesh-colored." He wrote that he "lost many a night's sleep" looking at the stars, but made it clear that he found this a special joy. Because he was so far south, he could see many stars that were not visible in Spain or Italy.

Amerigo and his crew met many Indians along the South American shore and in the Caribbean islands they visited at the end of their exploration. Some Indians asked the travelers into their homes, fed them, and gave them parrots, but others attacked the Europeans. Their armor and better weapons enabled Amerigo's men to win these battles. But Amerigo did something very wrong while exploring the Caribbean islands. He and his men seized over 200 Indians. They planned to convert them to Christianity and bring them back as slaves to Spain. Like Columbus and other Europeans of the time, Amerigo felt that the Indians would gain more by becoming Christians than they would lose by becoming slaves.

Amerigo, his men, and their captives sailed back home in the spring of 1500. They arrived in June of that year after a difficult voyage.

CHAPTER IV

AMERIGO'S GREAT VOYAGE

AMERIGO had made some important discoveries on his 1499 voyage, but neither he nor anyone else yet knew the truth about the land across the Atlantic Ocean. At the time, Amerigo may have thought he had explored Asia's fringes. Or, since the coast he had explored seemed different from the Asia described by people who had reached it on overland routes, perhaps he was puzzled by where he had been. In any event, Amerigo was very eager to return and learn more about the lands he had visited.

Almost immediately, Ferdinand and Isabella agreed to send Amerigo out with three ships. Amerigo faced a problem, however. During the late 1400s, Spain and Portugal had agreed to divide the lands in and across the Atlantic Ocean. The part of what is now Brazil that Amerigo wanted to visit was claimed by Portugal.

45

Amerigo couldn't legally explore it for Spain. We don't know exactly how, but Amerigo obtained permission from Ferdinand and Isabella of Spain and King Emanuel of Portugal to make a westward voyage of exploration for Portugal.

On May 13, 1501, Amerigo Vespucci sailed out of Portugal's capital city of Lisbon with three ships. This time he wanted to go south of his earlier exploration. After about two months at sea, the expedition reached Brazil, near the southernmost point Amerigo had reached on his 1499 voyage. From there the ships sailed south down the remaining length of Brazil.

Still heading south, Amerigo became the first known European to sail down the coast of present-day Uruguay. He then discovered the Plata River at the border of what are now Uruguay and Argentina, and also became the first known European to sail along Argentina's coast. Amerigo traveled down nearly the entire length of Argentina. If not for unfavorable weather, he might have sailed right through the Strait of Magellan, near South America's southern tip, and reached the Pacific Ocean. Had he done this, the Strait of Magellan, which the Portuguese explorer Ferdinand Magellan discovered almost twenty years later, in 1520, might have been named the Strait of Amerigo.

At a point not far from the Strait of Magellan, Amerigo turned toward home. As he sailed east, Amer-

Lisbon was a busy port in the fifteenth
and sixteenth centuries, with many ships
under construction and others being
readied for voyage.

igo carried something extremely valuable with him, although it wasn't a treasure such as gold or pearls. It was an idea, one of the most important ideas in history. The coast he had just explored could not possibly be Asia, Amerigo reasoned. It stretched several thousand miles too far south to be Asia. Instead, this landmass had to be a continent that lay between Europe and Asia. That explained why he and Columbus hadn't found any Asian cities, and why the Indians looked different from Asians. With this idea, Amerigo achieved his childhood goal of making a great discovery.

Upon his return to Lisbon in the summer of 1502, Amerigo wrote a letter to one of the Medicis, in which he expressed his momentous idea: ''We arrived at a new land which, for many reasons that are enumerated in what follows, we observed to be a continent.'' Amerigo's conclusion about the ''new land'' that was a ''continent'' quickly spread through Europe. He became identified in people's minds with this new continent.

CHAPTER V

TWO CONTINENTS ARE NAMED FOR AMERIGO

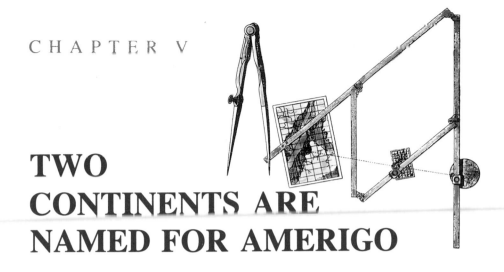

AMERIGO VESPUCCI lived ten more years after his return from his famous voyage. Soon after the voyage ended, he moved back to Seville, Spain. He married a Spanish woman, María Cerezo. Many honors were heaped upon Amerigo during his remaining years. In 1508, King Ferdinand (Queen Isabella had died in 1504) appointed him Chief Pilot of Spain. Ferdinand's papers appointing Amerigo to this grand position still exist.

Amerigo had two duties as Chief Pilot. First, he was a teacher. All sailors who wanted to be ship navigators had to visit Amerigo's home in Seville. Amerigo taught them how to use the astrolabe and the quadrant, as well as other things about ocean navigation. Amerigo awarded those who passed his test with a navigator's license.

Amerigo's second duty was to maintain Spain's official New World map. This was very important, be-

**Amerigo Vespucci, as the Chief Pilot
of Spain, was charged with keeping records
of discoveries in the New World.**

cause when Amerigo became Chief Pilot various maps were in use, many of them inaccurate. All pilots had to visit Amerigo before and after sailing to the New World. Those who were about to depart had to make a copy of Amerigo's official map, which was probably the most accurate New World map in existence. Returning pilots told Amerigo about places they had visited, enabling him to update the official map. Pilots who were caught using any map other than Amerigo's were fined.

Unfortunately, though, by this time Amerigo's health was poor. He had gotten malaria during his 1499 voyage to the New World. Recurring attacks of this disease slowly weakened him. On February 22, 1512, just a few days before what would have been his fifty-eighth birthday, Amerigo Vespucci died. With him at the end were his wife, María, and his nephew, Giovanni, whom he had taken under his wing much as his uncle Giorgio Antonio had done for him many years earlier.

Amerigo probably died without knowing about the greatest tribute to him. In 1507 several scholars in the town of Saint-Dié in northeastern France produced a book on geography and mathematics. Amerigo's discovery of a new continent was described in this book. The scholars coined a name for the continent, which until then had been called the ''Indies'' or the ''New World.'' Amerigo's name was *Americus* in Latin, which was the language of scholars. The scholars at Saint-Dié changed the

By 1520, when this world map was drawn, the name "America" was used by most mapmakers.

"us" at the end of "Americus" to "a" and called the continent America. They did this because the other known continents—Asia, Africa, and Europa (as Europe was then called)—all had names ending in "a." The scholars wrote: "I believe it should be named . . . after its discoverer, Americus, a wise man; or let it be named America, since both Europa and Asia bear feminine names."

People liked the sound of "America," and they also thought that Amerigo deserved to be honored for his discovery. By 1520 the name "America" had appeared on many maps and globes. Although North and South America are called separate continents, they are attached and could be called one huge continent. At first, just the part we call South America was called America. But in the years after Amerigo's death, the northern part also became known as America. To distinguish the two parts, people began calling them North America and South America.

THE MYSTERY OF AMERIGO VESPUCCI

Historians have argued about one aspect of Amerigo's life for centuries. A few of them think that Amerigo made two other major voyages to America in addition to the ones in 1499–1500 and 1501–02. The second of the two questionable voyages was supposedly made in 1503–04. This voyage supposedly took him back to the South American coast, but resulted in no major discoveries. However, the earlier voyage would be extremely important if it happened. On this voyage, which was said to have been made in 1497–98, Amerigo supposedly sailed up Mexico's eastern coast, continued eastward along what is now the United States' southeastern coast, rounded Florida, and then headed north all the way to the Virginia region.

Christopher Columbus is usually hailed as the first known European explorer to reach the American mainland after Leif Eriksson's voyage around A.D. 1000. Having explored only islands on his first two voyages to the New World, Columbus first reached the American mainland, in present-day Venezuela, on his third voyage in 1498. If Amerigo reached the North American coast in 1497, it means that he arrived at the mainland before Christopher Columbus!

Writings about these two questionable voyages were made in Amerigo's lifetime. But although Amerigo's name was on them, these writings obviously were not his. They contain many errors that Amerigo would not have made, and they are not in his writing style. Here is what may have happened. The people of 500 years ago liked adventure stories as much as we do. Writers may have made up exciting tales about Amerigo's trips to America and then put his name on them. Since there were no laws against this then, anyone's name could be put on a book.

On the other hand, would Amerigo have been given such important positions on his two known voyages if he had never sailed before? And would King Ferdinand have made him Chief Pilot on the basis of just two voyages? Perhaps Amerigo did make other voyages, but the writers who described them added imaginary details such as the possible exploration of the North American mainland. Unless more documents are found, this may always remain a mystery.

The imaginary or exaggerated writings on the two

A fifteenth-century artist presented this view of Vespucci with the caption: "Americus Vespuccius of Florence in a marvelous expedition to the West and to the South opened up two parts of the earth, greater than the shores which we inhabit and known to us in no previous age, one of which by common consent of all human beings is called by his name, America."

questionable voyages hurt Amerigo's reputation from the mid-1500s all the way to about the year 1900. Some scholars believed that Amerigo had written these himself. Some even claimed that everything Amerigo had written was imaginary, and that he had never reached America at all. A very few people even wanted to change the name of the American continents to Erikssonia in honor of Leif Eriksson, or Toscanelli in honor of a great Italian mapmaker who helped inspire Columbus's first voyage.

Can you imagine saying that you lived in "North Erikssonia" or saying "I pledge allegiance to the flag of the United States of Toscanelli"? But "America" isn't just a better name for the two continents because it sounds so lovely. Putting the two disputed voyages aside, the fact remains that Amerigo Vespucci was the first person to identify the lands across the Atlantic Ocean as an unknown continent. For this reason alone, isn't it fitting that North and South America were named for him?

GLOSSARY

Astrolabe—a very old instrument used to observe the positions of celestial bodies.

Coast—the land that lies along a large body of water.

Continent—our planet earth's biggest landmass.

Equator—the imaginary line that circles the east-west middle of the earth.

Expedition—a journey for a special purpose, or the group of people making that journey.

Malaria—a disease, spread by the bite of a certain mosquito, in which the patient suffers chills and fever.

Merchant—a person who buys and sells goods.

Navigation—controlling the course of a ship or airplane.

Quadrant—an old instrument used for measuring the positions of heavenly bodies.

Vikings—a people who lived in Norway and other Scandinavian lands in long-ago times.

FOR FURTHER READING

Arciniegas, Germán. *Amerigo and the New World*. New York: Alfred A. Knopf, 1955.

Fradin, Dennis Brindell. *Explorers: A New True Book*. Chicago: Childrens Press, 1984.

Lehner, Ernst, and Johanna Lehner. *How They Saw the New World*. New York: Tudor Publishing, 1966.

Lomask, Milton. *Great Lives: Exploration*. New York: Scribners, 1988.

Zweig, Stefan. *Amerigo: A Comedy of Errors in History*. New York: Viking Press, 1942.

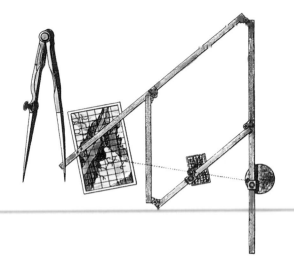

INDEX